PIANO • VOCAL • GUITAR

COME AND ADORE HIM
25 CCM Christmas Songs

ISBN 978-1-4584-0799-3

HAL•LEONARD®
CORPORATION

7777 W. BLUEMOUND RD. P.O. BOX 13819 MILWAUKEE, WI 53213

Visit Hal Leonard Online at
www.halleonard.com

contents

ADORE HIM

Words and Music by DON POYTHRESS
and TONY WOOD

Gentle Ballad

Count - less days on a
Ex - pec - ta - tion

jour - ney that led so far.
turned to ___ mys - ter - y,   for

Still, they bowed down.
hold - ing her child. }

Play 1st time only

Come, let us a - dore Him. O come, let us a -

dore Him. O come, let us a - dore Him.

dore Him.

CHRISTMAS THIS YEAR

Words and Music by TOBY McKEEHAN,
CARY BARLOWE and JESSE FRASURE

Recorded a half step lower.

just can't help but stop and grin; __ it's like I'm ten years old a-gain. __

And ev-'ry-where I go, __ I can feel it. Some say it moves __ like a spir-it.

It falls on us once a year, __ like it came on a mid-night __ clear.

The soul of this sea-son is __ a gift when love came down to let __ us live.

ALL BECAUSE A CHILD WAS BORN

Words and Music by MADELINE STONE
and CECE WINANS

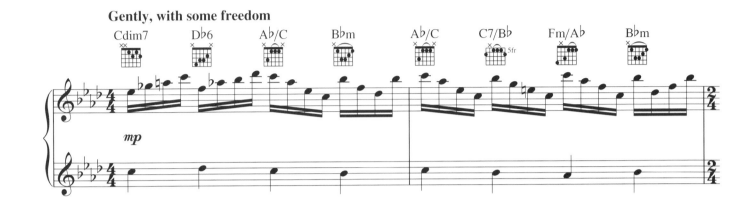

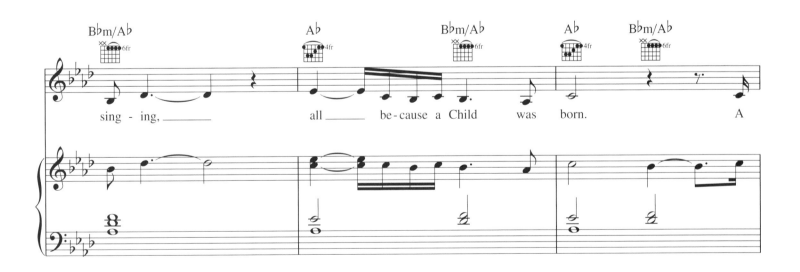

CHILD OF GOD

Words and Music by GRANT CUNNINGHAM
and MATT HUESMANN

FAMILY TREE

Words and Music by
DAVE BARNES

The fam - 'ly car; we bare - ly
rate with clum - sy
now; we all have

fit. Christ - mas time had come a -
hands, and hope that San - ta comes a -
changed, but we all laugh at the same old

EMMANUEL
(Hallowed Manger Ground)

Words and Music by CHRIS TOMLIN
and ED CASH

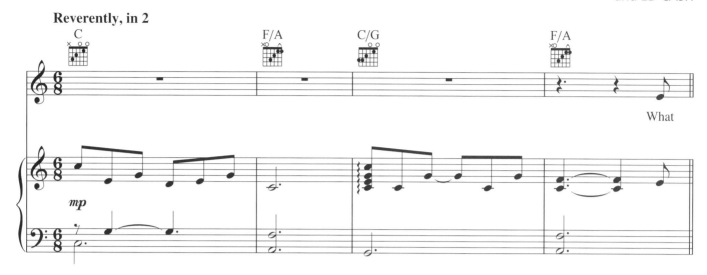

GIVE THIS CHRISTMAS AWAY

Words and Music by MATTHEW WEST
and SAM MIZELL

GLORIA

Words and Music by MICHAEL W. SMITH
Based on "Angels We Have Heard On High"

HE HAS COME FOR US

Words and Music by JASON INGRAM
and MEREDITH ANDREWS

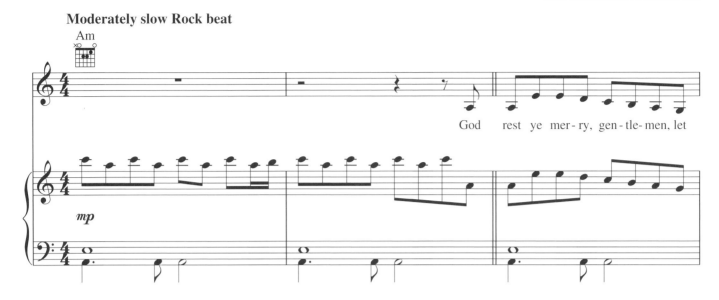

HALLELUJAH

Words and Music by
DARLENE ZSCHECH

Moderately slow

HARK! THE HERALD ANGELS SING/
THE MUSIC OF CHRISTMAS

Arranged by
STEVEN CURTIS CHAPMAN

I BELIEVE

Words and Music by
NATALIE GRANT

I HEARD THE BELLS ON CHRISTMAS DAY

Words by HENRY WADSWORTH LONGFELLOW
Additional Words and Music by MARK HALL,
DALE OLIVER and BERNIE HERMS

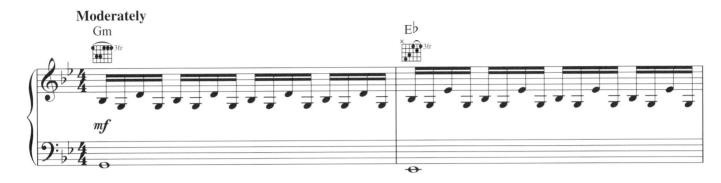

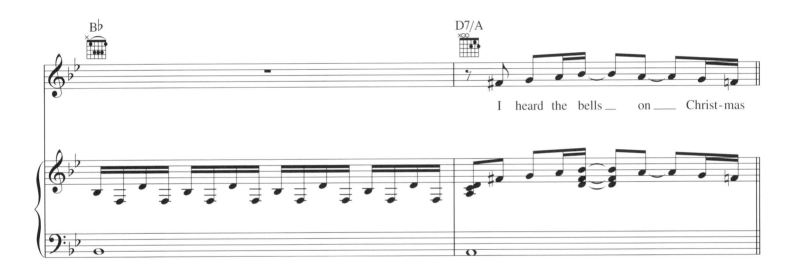

I heard the bells __ on __ Christ-mas

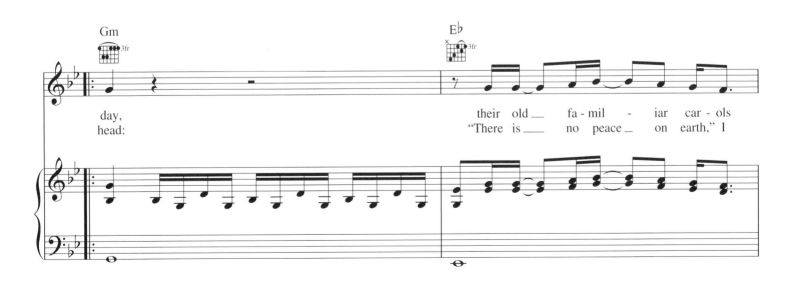

day,
head:

their old __ fa-mil-iar car-ols
"There is __ no peace __ on earth," I

I NEED A SILENT NIGHT

Words and Music by CHRIS EATON
and AMY GRANT

LAMB OF GOD

Words and Music by NICOLE C. MULLEN
and DAVID MULLEN

MESSIAH HAS COME

Words and Music by MARC BYRD
and STEVE HINDALONG

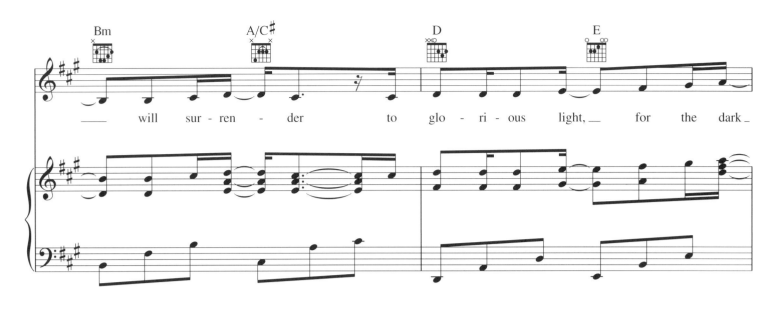

will sur - ren - der to glo - ri - ous light, __ for the dark __

will sur - ren - der to glo - ri - ous light. __

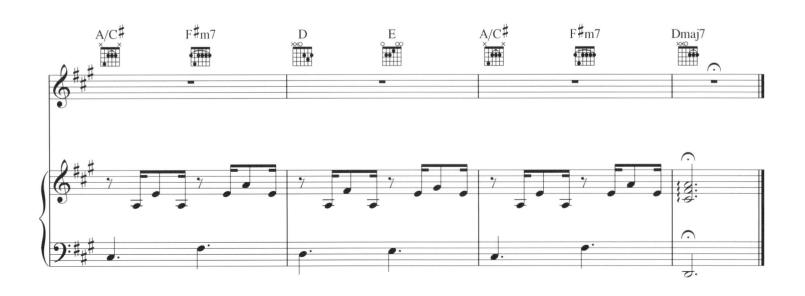

LIGHT OF THE WORLD

Words and Music by
MATT REDMAN

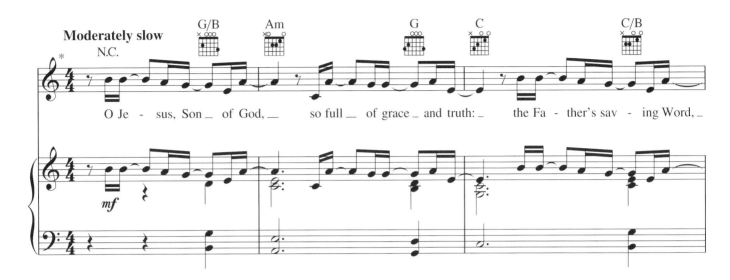

O Je - sus, Son _ of God, _ so full _ of grace _ and truth: _ the Fa - ther's sav - ing Word, _

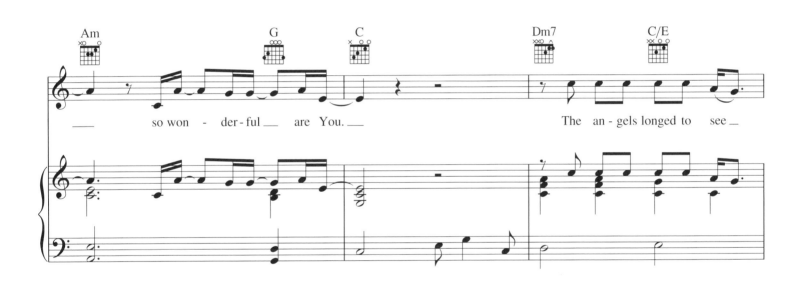

_ so won - der-ful _ are You. _ The an - gels longed to see _

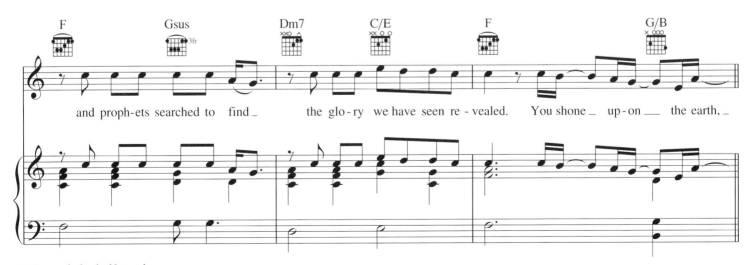

and proph-ets searched to find _ the glo - ry we have seen re - vealed. You shone _ up-on _ the earth, _

*Recorded a half step lower.

THE MIRACLE OF CHRISTMAS

Words and Music by
STEVEN CURTIS CHAPMAN

THE NIGHT BEFORE CHRISTMAS

Words and Music by LUKE BROWN,
CHUCK BUTLER and REGIE HAMM

THIS IS CHRISTMAS

Words and Music by JON MICAH SUMRALL
and DAVE LUBBEN

WHEN LOVE WAS BORN

Words and Music by STEPHANIE LEWIS,
BERNIE HERMS and MARK SCHULTZ

Recorded a half step lower.

WHERE'S THE LINE TO SEE JESUS?

Words and Music by STEVE HAUPT
and CHRIS LOESCH

365

Words and Music by DAVID MULLEN
and NICOLE MULLEN

WINTER SNOW

Words and Music by
AUDREY ASSAD

YOU GOTTA GET UP
(It's Christmas Morning)

Words and Music by
RICH MULLINS

More Contemporary Christian Folios from Hal Leonard
Arranged for Piano, Voice and Guitar

AVALON – THE GREATEST HITS
This best-of collection showcases 15 signature songs from throughout their career, plus a brand new tune soon to be fan favorite, the radio hit "Still My God." Includes: Adonai • Can't Live a Day • New Day • You Were There • and more.
00307056 P/V/G......................$17.99

THE JEREMY CAMP COLLECTION
A collection of 21 of this Dove Award-winner's best, including: Empty Me • Healing Hand of God • Jesus Saves • Let It Fade • Open Up Your Eyes • Right Here • Speaking Louder Than Before • Stay • Take You Back • There Will Be a Day • This Man • Walk by Faith • and more.
00307200 P/V/G......................$17.99

CASTING CROWNS – UNTIL THE WHOLE WORLD HEARS
Matching folio to the 2009 release featuring 11 songs from this Christian pop group: Always Enough • Joyful, Joyful • At Your Feet • Holy One • To Know You • Mercy • Blessed Redeemer • and more.
00307107 P/V/G $16.99

STEVEN CURTIS CHAPMAN – BEAUTY WILL RISE
Matching folio to Chapman's touching release that was written in response to the death of one of his daughters. 12 songs, including: Just Have to Wait • Faithful • Heaven Is the Face • I Will Trust You • and more.
00307100 P/V/G $16.99

DAVID CROWDER*BAND – CHURCH MUSIC
Our matching folio to the innovative 2009 release features 17 tunes, including the hit single "How He Loves" and: All Around Me • Can I Lie Here • Oh, Happiness • Shadows • We Are Loved • What a Miracle • and more.
00307089 P/V/G......................$17.99

NATALIE GRANT – LOVE REVOLUTION
All 11 songs from the 2010 CD by this multi-Dove Award winner. Includes her latest hit single "Human" and: Beauty Mark • Daring to Be • Desert Song • The Greatness of Our God • Love Revolution • Power of the Cross • Someday Our King Will Come • Song to the King • You Deserve • Your Great Name.
00307164 P/V/G......................$16.99

BRANDON HEATH – LEAVING EDEN
Matching folio to Dove Award-winning artist Brandon Heath's newest release. 11 tracks, including: As Long As I'm Here • It's Alright • It's No Good to Be Alone • The Light in Me • Might Just Save Your Life • Now More Than Ever • The One • Stolen • Your Love • and more.
00307208 P/V/G......................$16.99

HILLSONG LIVE – A BEAUTIFUL EXCHANGE
All 13 songs from the chart-topping 19th album in the live praise & worship series from Australia's Hillsong Church. Contains: Beautiful Exchange • Believe • Forever Reign • Like Incense • Love like Fire • The One Who Saves • Open My Eyes • Our God Is Love • Thank You • You • and more.
00307188 P/V/G......................$16.99

THE BEST OF JOHN P. KEE
This great compilation offers 14 favorites from this North Carolina-based gospel singer/songwriter in piano/vocal format complete with choir vocals. Includes: The Anointing • He'll Welcome Me • I Do Worship • Jesus Is Real • Mighty God • Show Up! • Strength • Wash Me • and more.
00306997 Vocal/Piano w/Choir Vocal Harmonies...$17.99

KUTLESS – IT IS WELL
Matching folio to the second worship album from these Christian rockers, featuring 12 songs, including: Everything I Need • God of Wonders • Redeemer • What Faith Can Do • and more.
00307099 P/V/G $16.99

NICOLE C. MULLEN – THE ULTIMATE COLLECTION
Features a complete retrospective of this beloved Dove Award-winner's body of work. 20 terrific songs in all, including: Always Love You • Call on Jesus • Everyday People • Faith, Hope & Love • I Wish • On My Knees • Redeemer • Talk About It • more!
00307131 P/V/G......................$17.99

RECOLLECTION: THE BEST OF NICHOLE NORDEMAN
This 17-song collection features the finest releases from this popular CCM singer/songwriter, plus two new songs — "Sunrise" and "Finally Free." Includes: Brave • Fool for You • Real to Me • River God • This Mystery • and more.
00306633 P/V/G......................$17.95

PHILLIPS, CRAIG & DEAN – THE ULTIMATE COLLECTION
31 songs spanning the career of this popular CCM trio: Favorite Song of All • Hallelujah (Your Love Is Amazing) • I Want to Be Just Like You • Shine on Us • Your Grace Still Amazes Me • and more.
00306789 P/V/G $19.95

SWITCHFOOT – THE BEST YET
This greatest hits compilation features the newly released song "This Is Home" and 17 other top songs. Includes: Concrete Girl • Dare You to Move • Learning to Breathe • Meant to Live • Only Hope • Stars • and more.
00307030 P/V/G $17.99

TENTH AVENUE NORTH – THE LIGHT MEETS THE DARK
The very latest from this Florida CCM band contains 11 songs, the hit single "Healing Begins" and: All the Pretty Things • Any Other Way • Empty My Hands • House of Mirrors • Oh My Dear • On and On • Strong Enough to Save • The Truth Is Who You Are • You Are More.
00307148 P/V/G......................$16.99

THIRD DAY – MOVE
All 12 songs from the just-released CD by these award-winning Christian rockers. Includes the hit single "Lift Up Your Face" and: Children of God • Everywhere You Go • Follow Me There • Gone • I'll Be Your Miracle • Make Your Move • Sound of Your Voice • Surrender • Trust in Jesus • What Have You Got to Lose.
00307186 P/V/G......................$16.99

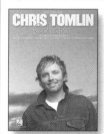

THE CHRIS TOMLIN COLLECTION
15 songs from one of the leading artists and composers in contemporary worship music, including the favorites: Amazing Grace (My Chains Are Gone) • How Great Is Our God • Indescribable • We Fall Down • and more.
00306951 P/V/G......................$16.99

THE BEST OF CECE WINANS
14 favorite songs from the gospel superstar: Alabaster Box • He's Always There • It Wasn't Easy • Looking Back at You • Pray • Purified • Throne Room • What About You • and more.
00306912 P/V/G $16.99